Drinking Girls and Their Dresses

ahsahta press

The New Series

number 2

Drinking Girls and Their Dresses

poems by

Heather Sellers

ahsahta press

Boise State University • Boise, Idaho • 2002

AHSAHTA PRESS, BOISE STATE UNIVERSITY
BOISE, IDAHO 83725
http://ahsahtapress.boisestate.edu

Printed in the United States of America
Cover art: "The Self-Destructive Optimist" by Laurie Lipton
    (http://www.laurielipton.com)

First printing 2002
ISBN 0-916272-74-5

Library of Congress Cataloging-in-Publication Data

Sellers, Heather, 1964-
Drinking girls and their dresses : poems / by Heather Sellers.
    p. cm. -- (Ahsahta Press new series ; no. 2)
ISBN 0-916272-74-5 (pbk. : alk. paper)
I. Title. II. Series.
PS3569.E5749 D75 2002
811'.6--dc21

                                    2002007859

For R.S., in memory

Dr. Mosher thinks that standing continually with the weight on the left foot is more injurious than bearing it on the right foot, for it causes the uterus and ovaries to press upon the rectum. An effort should be made to call her thoughts to other themes.

—"What a Young Woman Ought to Know,"
Mary Wood-Allen, M.D., 1913

Contents

Acknowledgments

I am grateful to Brenda Hillman for generously helping this manuscript along. I am indebted to the Spunky Monkeys— Jane Bach, Greg Rappelye, Jack Ridl. Thanks also to David DeZwaan, Kate ten Haken, Jackie Bartley, Jill Heydt-Stevenson, and Ann Turkle.

The Ragdale Foundation, Hawthornden, The Seaside Institute, St. Lawrence University, the Viebranz House, and Hope College supported the completion of this manuscript by providing time, space, and community.

Grateful acknowledgment to the editors at the following magazines, who published the poems in this collection, sometimes in different versions: *Barrow Street, Field, Gulf Coast, Hawaii Review, Indiana Review, The Journal, The Midwest Quarterly, The New Orleans Review, The New Virginia Review, Primavera,* and *Sonora Review.*

Judge's Note

"Heather Sellers' poems make accounts that undo themselves;
they alternate a smooth, confident syntax with lurching,
skidding rhythms to made dark and funny models of the
'unacceptable' cultures within cultures of American life: 'We are
frantic families here. We are all bitten up,' she begins. Her Florida
is an intense, extra-surreal lining to the dream Wallace Stevens
had of it. I am drawn to her large-spirited and elegiac depictions
of humans with doomed fates and retread futures. Her free-verse
line argues with its freedoms, a jaggedness as agitated as a coast
that is loved and feared."

Brenda Hillman
Judge, Sawtooth Poetry Prize

Drinking Girls and Their Dresses *was a runner-up for the Sawtooth*
Poetry Prize 2002.

Being from Orlando

We are frantic families here. We are all bitten up.
The lawns have red frosting for flowers, the flowers
have teeth for pistils. They're not really from around
here. Nothing from around here, not even the water or us,
the people. We vote yes to flamingoes by the highways,
we fling bread at them on the way to the Grapefruit Mall.

And we want
flowers that grow on linen skirts and English china.
Orlando used to be called Mellonville, used to be infested
with pests. Shuffleboard, croquet, lawn bowling. Plumosa,
cabbage palms, banana and bamboo. Hibiscus here
is a spicy weed, not a pricey exotic, we rip the stuff
out of the back yard and burn it.

My hair is wet underneath
from March through November. I save a
drowning boy, being from Orlando. My
brother swims in the Junior Olympics. My mother
swims across a lake when she is angry
at my father. She wears her clothes.
She swims for three hours.

Year after year we ski around
Orlando, in between Orlando, all the lakes,
blue pads of cool, some bottomless, some so
brown from pine needles unfolding, they stain
the whites of your eyes til Christmas. We thread

our way through the wet blue heart. We think surely
it will sink, this city of admirals, tangelos and panama
hats, this city with its men in white guyaberas.

We are from Orlando. We don't like to be too dry.
We have returned to our houses still standing, our citrus
which cannot taste us, and our lakes have returned to soup.
They are melding together. We are trading places. We are
going North to go to school, we are heading South to work
in maritime museums, on the beach. Being away from Orlando
we see we were visiting the place, in its sky blue uniform. It's a hotel
for fruit, a winter tempo with a hurricane for every girl, and,
in every room by noon a little bit of the sea we lived for.

Polar

I might just have to drown you children
I might just drown us all.
No, my brother and I said. We were blonde
and forceful, planning
on snack, children of our own, the beach.
My mother's face was voile. Florida
was green felt and eggshells, fingernails
and rind. Hurricanes were relaxing to me.
I thought of them as marriages.
My body was a swizzle stick. My mind a
rainy crash. You children eat a lot.
My mother's chin was a goose.
She smelled like sweat. I pretended
to be a baby when she wasn't around.
I dispersed myself when she was.
Don't ever let me hear you say the word God,
she said. Now, she is quiet and old and fluid
like a conch. She looks out upon the bottomless
Lake Underhill in Orlando, a gray lake
refusing to reflect the sky, a pale water
that shadows what's to come. Most of the
time she doesn't remember or invent.
You two were never spanked, she says.
I'm still falling. But I do not think in opposites.
I always knew better than that, not that.

Over Oranges

I'm eating apples now but thinking of oranges
sticky peels like tongues in our palms.
I'm dreaming bougainvillea and hibiscus dreams,
I think I'm pink and buggy still.
But I live in Detroit and the park across the street
has orange arms reaching down, and brushing.
It's over. The leaves are salty. I make the bed
to keep it quiet, to keep it
pressing its skin and sandy smells.
I'm ready. October is all one yesterday,
is a milky gray cloud with frayed edges
moving fast in the north sky.
Erasing.

When Lost Was Better

I was seven, into
pinafores, pickles and
keeping my hair
wet, a fussy swimming
girl, bad with numbers,
happy marrying words,
making many basic desserts,
I lost my cross, my good
gold cross, in the yard,
maybe in the sink or at
the grocery store, in the green
tile aisles. My mother thought
I lost it in church, on the patio
outside Father Stephen's office.
Nope, I said. I was never standing
there. That April I lost
my pet bird Miss Kelly Green,
my report card, my abilities
to stay quiet for hours at a stretch.
I lost my temper, enjoyed
flailing. I lost my brother's doll,
my mom's plaid jacket, her house keys,
a dollar and my sleeping bag.
I turned eleven, lost everything.
Now strong, tan, long-legged,
blonde as batter, tall

as heaven and my arms
thin as tails, I found, shining
in the thick new mowed
backyard tarzan grass, my cross,
the tiny grooved piece
of metal, lawnmower chewed and spit
out, my cross in the shape
of an asterisk. I said to myself:
Heather, you are a martyr in shorts
and white sandals at Cherokee Indian
Junior High in Orlando.
I kept the chewed-up cross in my
jewelry box, on a cushion.
But I wish the cross was still lost;
I liked the years looking, missing better.
Lost is lost.
And is like faith, because broken
kept longer and more dearly, in the pink
box in the girl bedroom opposite the
memory of the grandmother, with coins.
And pearls. You don't lose the dead,
they lose you.

Underwater

Well, we are underwater here and I am worried, my
mother says on the phone from Florida this morning.
How're your dogs? How are your headaches? she asks
me and then she says let me call you right back your
phone bills are going to be astronomical.

Then there is depression and grey clouds. Then there are
the dogs, rolling in poop as frequently as possible.
My friends are sick of hearing about my love letters
To El Niño. Then there is the sun's going out one day, which
makes me feel a little bit better about dying, but not much.

I have been working on my spine, teaching it to breathe.
My sister is in the hospital, receiving electro-convulsive therapy.
The shocking gives her headaches, which makes her crazy. And
her mother who is also my mother says I don't mean to leave
in a hurry. Okay. But I can't be two places at once.

The quark guy on the radio is interested in what
everybody else is doing. In his studio in Santa Fe, he sees
no difference between the stock market and the immune system.
Be rich and healthy? I want to scream. How is the dog doing?
He is marking his territory. He is suggesting fear and worry.

You can't be two places at once? You are always two places
at once. That's your baseline, baby, that is called The Walking
Dead. The problem is this: those of us who are paying attention,
I mean really paying attention are thousands of places at a time,
there's more. In a deep dark blue warm sea. I am, we are

one eye on the tiniest of the peculiar glowing fish.

Ocean Pacific

My other brother spent his last winter
Making—sanding, heating glass, sanding—surfboards

In our carport where the green breeze and
Corrugated roof rippled his wide forehead, his bare face.

This was the boy who once drank gas—only a drop
Or seven, enough to stipple a throat. Not the one you've had

Beer with. The other brother. At ease with the forest under his palms.
Free from the father, the dungeons, the bikes, babes, the lords, the doom.

His name was Sean. We called him seen. Green machine.
But he wasn't. He made surfboards, old boards, long boards. For friends.

For free. Sheltered, like a car, probably exhausted in the carport and
Thirsty. An oily fixture bent layering, shaving, waxing his boards.

Mostly bending what couldn't be bent. Sand, sea, the big bed of ocean.
My brother lived to slide and fall and loop. He never wore a leash.

He could breathe only under the green translucence of carport, or
In the sun, at the Cape. I catch the smell though, when I am at the mall

Or the coast. I smell the crusty cap of seawater blonde hair,
        fused, a cuttlebone.
He had friends. He sensed the falling was inevitable

Was an asking for a fast back to stand on forever.
A winged bullet, a sword with a fin.

(Me, I'm the sister with one sticky foot, arms—wings—water for crying.
I know the sweetest fruit is at the top of the tree, and I know why, sun.)

Bucky Ditched Me

Bucky ditched me starboard.
Seagreen Irish eyes and only two
Lies. I love you, and I love you.
Bucky ditched me in the grass.
Into the blue dishes and pine needles,
ditched me for Angela Ball,
for Charlie X, for a sail, for a sky.
I said sorry, I said sweets.
I said Bucky ditch me right here
Right now. Say my hair is beautiful
is your Sleeping chains. Say anything.
I'm old. I'm sad. When Bucky held
me, sea cold arms. I leaped. I thought
she leapt for joy. When I was her.

Florida Fifth Grade

Mr. Rowe let us play the stock market
with fake money and real newspapers for six
weeks and we were never so happy. Never
before had I talked. Now I was rolling, rich, laughing
with boys, a lot. I even jumped on the seat of
my desk when my Coca Cola split. Then we learned
Mr. Rowe didn't really wear glasses, he sold real
estate to old women from Chicago, women who all
died, faded or something before the movers
came for their breakfronts, hutches and goods. And a fourteen
year old girl was pregnant. We weren't afraid.
We weren't going to her junior high, we were a feeder
school for downtown, and our Rowe wore yellow shirts,
smelled like apples, and said "You are the best class
I've ever had. You kids are going high places." We held
our complex sums and our ticker tapes; everything was
frozen and streaming at once, the Big Crash. We felt
guilty, like it was us. "I wasn't cheating," Andrew
Snedeker said. "It was Eric." I said we could be quieter.

"At least he wasn't trying to stuff religion into you,"
my mother said. Like Mr. Godfrey, my history
teacher, with pink girl twins who had to be spanked,
yes, babies, spanked, hard, so they'd know he loved them and their
baptism meant something. "I cry right with them," he said,
"Sometimes harder." Godfrey was bald, gleaming. White
shirts, dark suits. "Know Jesus," he said. "Know Him and love Him."

Once I saw Mr. Godfrey. I was walking
late to lunch from the library. He was crying,
secretly softly banging his head on the cement
wall of the cafetorium, around back, his shiny patent
shoes like badgers in the sticker
grass and weeds. Around back by the
dumpsters. He didn't look like he knew
anyone. I was getting a B.

The Empress of Ties

Dede started a tie company.
In our town men wore bathing
Suits. No one bought neckties.
We were invited to hot tub parties.
We drank wine in our hand-beaded
Culottes on the beach. We made
Two men red silk thongs. We watched
A lot of All My Children. Dmitri wore
Sulka ties. We admired his bias and drape.
Wal-mart opened, and then closed
In our little town. Bob Lawson had a real
Nervous breakdown, and prison.

The last day of our lease, we tied all the ties,
Maybe a hundred silk striped green and gold,
Pink and purple, black and yellow ties,
The Emperor's New Clothes
Was closing. The lizard ties, the electric tie,
The wood tie, the piano keys tie, the clear plastic,
Fishbones tie. We knotted and pinned one long ribbon
Of silk and artifact, tied it first around Dede's waist,
Tied it around my waist and she took off
On her bike.
When she was far enough ahead that the line
Was taut and the ties were stretched
The town was suddenly noticing we were the gals

Who made ties. We rode down Monroe Street
Linked with our ribbon of ties, up Tennessee, out Apalachee
Parkway. Men came out of their casual wayward offices,
Stood between their wrinkled cars, stared.
They were feeling a blankness, a space, a stripe
Of emptiness on their chests. For the first time.

We rode to the coast, married like that, on our last day.
And when we arrived on the sand, we unleashed ourselves,
Released the stripe of our year of sewing madness.
We flung our ties up, into the wind, a tail. A pelican
Grabbed the red crimson glory tie by its
Neck, and our long silky V breaking apart, he flew slowly
Over the marshy gulf, into the Florida sky, which was oxford shirt
Blue, a placket of white cirrus.

Concert

Tonight I watch boys push up the moon, spill
madras drink. In a moment you will
arrive in stolen telephone
wire hair, a dress of black petals shirred down
your bare back.

We want our lovers to taste December, amber,
these nights with kitchens of stars. Just for fun?
you ask, pulling our bright squeeze into concert.
Yes, yes, I say, dancing, fearing arrest, the end

music which wants us sleeping.
Can we get closer? I wish, kissing
my last green penny, my little car, the ravine
out back where finally we will part like
hats on night thick seas.

Perfect World

His closet is quiet as grass,
All the ambitious greens cool blue,
Shrunk to fit.

You have met him and the kiss
Is shiraz, bit of a cosseted tilt, a must.
You will never become full of this guy.

He is the guy, the one, is this: the best of furniture,
Drama, faith and hibiscus, weedy sturdy stuff.
I'm being silly now. But you know or smell:

The combinations, they are endless and
Maybe you know that is the definition of hope.
Endless combinations. So I descend, into what is his.

It's like a song I'm making up as I go-go.
Carry a tune, can't carry a tune, that's not
Innate, it comes. It goes. The way of the weather.

Like seasons. Like amphibians. Like this love.
Trash day, or your fixation on brown or Sweden.
But, always: Give me some more. This is where I lie now.

And I'll send this one little emissary into his long sleeves:

Remembering when I was a child, flat on my father's lawn
Convex to the sky, the coat of wool, horn buttons, the topper,
That'll be me, inside out; of you, that'll be you, but who?

From shoes to hat to box. Love, a little closet—we have one of these—
In the house of darkness. Don't now know. We are somehow
Finding what to pick from that deep seduction of such a tiny place.
    And it's a muscle.

Beauty and the Beast

I'll be the beast.

So I kiss my dog on the
lips. His velvet
weatherstripping
pulls, stays, parts
like the black lips
I keep pretty
secret. He tastes
like burnt sugar.

My ears waver and peel
back. I cannot help myself.

I want to marry
my little dog, the boy
princess. My counter-
tenor hound singing
missa, picking roses,
floating down the candle-
lit hallways in his fur capes.
This is my fairy tale, my Disney
way of dreaming up.

I am toothy and whiskered,
merle and nearly gleaming
in my animal presence.

And my palms are smoking.
Always a little fresh from my kill.

Belle-o, please bark at me.
Please stand on my body and quiver.
Could you bless me, sanctify me?
Your arrows, my claws.
Am I disturbing you?
I could be Diana. I could be
your tiny alert shadow.

The Sock Symbol

Here is a photo of
my boyfriend putting on
his shoes. Sitting on the pier,
shaking sand out
of his sock. The sock
is out in front of him,
a blurry confusion. He's trying
to shirk it. He wants
to talk tonight on the
phone to a woman in
San Diego. He doesn't
know why. That's all unclear.

I have the wrong hand in focus,
the still side of him.
I have clear only the arm
holding him back, a cable
of containment. He
leans away, out of my depth
of field and flaps
the sock. On his foot
light says a benediction.

I have great hopes for this
photo, for the sock that
leaps back to me bent wrong

and rubbery, a caught fish.
Let me catch you silly and
keep this: that dumb sock,
your face a dune, on the boards,
under the bench, your other sock
balled in its shoe, a dark moon
in a dark suede boat; you'll
shake that one too. It won't
bear fruit. It won't mean
anything. Except a little
less sand on those frosty feet.

Entrance

I heard a fly buzz when I got
married. I heard a song playing lyrics
I will always know the way you know
something right after it is said.

He says I remind him of Piltdown girl.
That hurts like hogwash, I take it with a tumbler
of salt. She's fake! Not even a girl, you know.
My car needs new brakes. My house needs

New light. My tub is like your love is, over-
flowing. It's a long way down. Everyone
knows how to cry. It's a long way to
your ear. This is why we got married,

We need ears to lick, ears to reflect our noses and
we need palms to press, cash to flash. A boy has
a certain smell and he gets hungry for cookies,
too! The complete package. We need this bliss of

Not-thinking, the stupor of oneness. Marriage is stupor elevated.
I always thought I would just marry Florida, or maybe
a state of mind. Flesh comes as a surprise, your crazy
needles (I remind you of Piltdown girl?) kip and

Keep me. Okay. The sun is strong after the
wedding. You sleep in our bed in the shape
of a K. I wander around the downstairs
hungry and homesick. The dog has written his own

Vows. We confer on the back steps, two
breaths on the stoop, the door open wide.
The dog has written in a lot of walking.
I have to give this pause, I say. What I see

On my wedding day: in our garden, and I must
add, in the select garden next door to us, the hyacinths, hard
knobs of wet silk, black and stinky. The snails are
smart. Cloak, and eat. The snails are making themselves

Into plump shiny awnings over all these awesome back-door deaths.

When I Was Worried I Was Pregnant

My body filled with trees and wind.
Branches scraped the more marmoreal
parts of me at night and during the day
I walked around with two eyes black
and blue from worrying. And I imagined
that little baby fucked up and bossing
me. But I don't want to leave my body
behind. That will come soon enough.
There's another way. A slide in behind
the screen of these days, light that
comes from inside fruit all summer,
and as the riches drop and spoil, slowly
let the body be lifted up, lighter, lighter

Belly Water Midnight Easy

1.

Jane, midwife of blackberry patch and friends with tangled
mid-sections, you stop, when you're trimming canes,
flex the ribbons of purple, touch the good red to your tongue.
You're old, just slightly crabby and peach at the edges. Evening.
That's your favorite time of all. A space in the woman's afternoon
where the day runs like water, silvery and easy.

2.

My friend Jane, untangled; you ready us for morning.
You've given me a name for every baby in me. This new baby, your
    daughter's
Son, is nothing new for you. A dollop of friendliness:
He's the cherry on top. You've had lives in lives cased in
Echoes since before you were born, all your eggs rich, all those plenties.
All your good thinking! Just thinking. Jane, you're my brainy body.
(And Baby Mogan's a well-run small hotel on a cotton backroad.)

3.

You're my favorite tree. A real fine kind of zone seven heaven.
Table Mountain pine, I think, abundant cones, egg-shaped, opening
Partly at maturity; remaining attached for many years.
As we thicken and keel, as babies' babies tuft and meddle
And needle their trouty selves westward, sweet as strawberries, I'm
Always reseeding you in me, Jane. Growing the good gifts
you've left behind the hedge of me. Pine, candles, milk.

Your Foyer, Sunday Afternoon, December

I see you have cactus now,
sitting in a red clay dish—
a village of cacti, all kinds,
the anemone, the phallus
with spines, the skinny
phallus without spines,
the phallus with a red bloom,
the creeping snakes. Quietly
stationed on a circular sofa
of bitty white ground stones.
On the good wood chest. With
no saucer underneath. I won't
say anything. I'm still sorry
I called your azalea
planting "the killing fields."
I see the floor is clean, the way
you like it, cold tile shining.

I've been away, winded,
popular and stuffing myself.
I started thinking of you the way
one starts thinking of a drink
about 3 in the afternoon during
difficult, summer or midlife
spells. I started thinking Scrabble.
Jeopardy. Côte du Rhône.

Cheap. I started thinking,
grocery store on Saturday
afternoon with your calm
thinking of Triscuits, low
fat with jack and that roasted
pesto stuff in the small green jar,
a tiny glass pouch of green ground leaves.

Cactus grow so slowly, you see
them in years. When I was un-
ravelling a sweater on Nob Hill
(my teeth weren't sleepy) were
you beyond this foyer, were you
moving letters around, or rinsing?
Do I just want, and then keep
wanting? When I was lying on white
linen sheets alone in a desolate hotel,
cool steamy green hills, a little canyon palace
of sorrow, with my knees in my breasts,
my head an ocean of mixtures, did you
think, at that moment, I will buy a dish
with a city of stones and succulents,
I will put away my Buddha, I'll put away
my cross—the dresser must be different
now. The Saturday gray sweater needs
other pants? Did you sit in your office
chair at the dining room table and think:
my spoiled love. Her needles, weeping.

Nebraska

Another dutiful another great Plains sunset,
cranberry and wine. We play good Westerners
hidebound by cattle money, Anger Management
class, a hankering to be More Badlands. "Kansas—
it's windy because Oklahoma sucks and Nebraska
blows."

Deck of Cards

I can't hear you, my husband
says. "I can't understand the words
coming out of your mouth."
Are you crazy, I am saying
to him. [Shopping, the clothes
smell of bleach, colors sorted out,
a hot steering wheel,] desire is my goal.
At the casino, Kewadin, What are
You Kewadin For, the gamblers
are women and the women are depressed
from ages five through ninety five.
There are women in wheelchairs
and bonnets and there is a woman in
a wedding dress, crackling. There's
breath, pink wine at the slot machines.
Their husbands are pineapples. Their
fingernails are rind. Let's go home, I
say. Good luck on the ace, he says.
Swallow, and reach. That's all we do
these days. Share a bathroom.
Get rid of an infection. Radiance?
I was thinking sunshine and eggplant,
I was thinking sand, dust, ocean, elapsing.
A small brown and white dog there,
maybe in the middle of a clean sweep.
I didn't say anything. I wasn't saying
anything, I just decided, at all.
But that was all after.
I spoke

A Dream I Had After An Environmental Mass

One morning I was out walking.
I saw hot red pokers, foxglove,
angelica, and a van with two
ruddy curly strong men in it.
I ate salmon later, and drank
beer with some mussels and
when I left Poltonhall I was
thinking of Toad Hall and that's
how I got to the frogs.

I always get back to the frogs.
I want them all back. That
night I read Wendell Berry poems,
they are harder than you think.
I work in the kitchen, brush
my long dark hair into lateral creases
and I dread death.

And so You Take a Leap into the

> Dr. Pengelly, Kalamazoo—Dear Sir: the Woman's Friend, now
> Zoa-Phora, is my friend because it relieved my wife in her
> last two confinements of the unutterable agony which
> attended her first labor. She used the Friend for about one
> month previous to expectant confinement, and to use her
> own language, "would not be without it for the world."

> —A COMPENDIUM OF FACTS RELATING TO
> WOMAN'S PHYSICAL NATURE
> DETROIT, 1882

I have so many inquiries concerning these complaints.
I think it best to devote. My heart is yours. At least one full chapter.
A part of this book. We think it best to devote. I love
your shoulders, your gold eyes, fire across the little lake, our walk
up the mown hill to the tower. Intelligence and common
sense are the best medicines. The vagina is a post, a pillar
on which the uterus stands, that pear, supported by so many guy ropes.
The woman's friend is ersatz. The agony is hard to digest.
The woman's friend tastes terrible, a child you do not care for.
This motion agitates the juices. I have a hand that remembers your warm
hand. The woman's friend is the man in love with her.
Irregular Sunday habits make irregular bowels.
I don't want to go to church with you. I want to make love, read the paper,
turn the leftover salmon into eggs, add a little bit of pepper.
I am angry. This practice results in irritation, which craves more

rubbing. Let me use my own language.
She says, "she can't bear to tinker with herself."
I have so many questions regarding love. A sulky plow.
Is my friend. Many a man provides himself
with convenient barns and outbuildings, a self-binder.
It involves not the uterus alone, but the whole system.

Widow's Peak

When I would pull hairs out of it, my mother
said it's your signature, don't erase it. Okay,
I said, a sign of terrible, awesome beauty.
Well anyway better than a mole, like your
babysitter has, why your father loves those
things, I do not know. They can sprout
hairs. I didn't believe anything she told me.

She told me I inherited my widow's peak
from my grandmother up north, the vee of dark hair in
the center of my forehead, Frankenstein hoodlet.
Ugly-pretty, my mother always said, of plastic
flowers, sculpted shag, velvet capes, shiny black
vinyl couches and caps, my favorite things.

Venus doesn't have one. It's not a fair
thing. Or, take the Mona Lisa—looks a bit
bald to those of us with the widow's peak.

Last week I learned provenance of the name.
I had always thought, just below the level
of thought, in a crooked way, that the widow
part wasn't significant, it was the peak one
got with this particular hairline. The peak,
I had a peak, I was at peak, a pinnacle of beauty.

The widow's peak is a sign your husband
will die and soon. Fishwives in France
turned up peaked, men drowned, and my
grandmother, my Alsace-Lorraine grandmother, lost
her husband, Buck Keating, when she was 34,
the age I will be next year. He wasn't fishing,
he wasn't in France. He was golfing at North
Shore. But still. He died, she was
peaked and I have hers. I am looking
for my husband but I can see now
why he is hiding from me. Marked man.

What You Should Not

I'll tell you what. I'll tell you now and then
I am going. I was sleeping. You were dreaming.
I'm living twice, cleanly. You were pressing a
cool mouth to my thigh, up. Up.

Not like music: your song of me in shapes, song baby
dreams, pop portico, Miss Pepita song, rock song,
the little dog rocks baby too. No, you can't you see me.
Like a rainstorm, like a rattle. I'll tell you what. I'm awake. Isn't

That how it began? I can also envision someone else's
lover, blue sheets and the older son who looked.
Coupla little leaps, boom boom, sunlight kind of prickled
and squeaking. Not that it's all come out in the wash. What you

Do is this. Stay. Or go. Two years from now, we'll still have the packets
of spices you brought from the West, adult skin, your arrow maybe
humming, sticky jag in the time zone, bullets and dances. Know that
If I were a bed, and, also, slept in, I'd let you keep your children here.

April Sunburn

The first, my skin brand
new on me, tight
not washed out.
I'm something other to touch:
scales, something good—hot
sweet blister like citrus rind.

Where my necklace was,
the dove charm now
a white-winged hole
above my breasts
where a little light, my one
rubbed away place, beams.

The sun that gave it to me I love.
The word sunburn strangely smoothes,
a blinding kiss from the sky.
I can write on myself, I do,
you can, too. The burned skin
thirsts for letters, swallows.

Better than a new dress, sun
burn lasts four days.
I'm busy with night, the cut
flowers falling, love, ice.
Four days
to use up that fire.

Big Quiet Space in the Bed for Almost an Hour at Midnight

The lover and I are lying squarely
in the queen-size bed. The covers are
not warm. We are not alone. The dog
has no pupils, he's all iris, prince, and pant,
those brown earths rolling around
above a great dividing grin. What
stands between us? He's got that
wild-eye look—the rubber teeth showing.
The dog looks so hot and crazy.
Like a mad red thought, he will not
get off the bed. And we will not,
either. Because we are talking. You
are digging your heels in. The mattress
pushes my back like a terrible idea,
looming. I feel like I am standing up.
In the dead center of my life. Hello,
dog, uncalm. No, this is not relaxing
at all, is it. He will not look me in
the eye. You hate this, don't you, dog,
Discussion is no god you'd consider
omnipotent. Would it be bad to read
the *Atlantic* article on chaos now? dog
asks. I wonder, breathing. Happy I am
like a man. There's some promise there.
And the dog is like a boy, difficult and spiny
eventually sweet, like a long book. The dog
is a pineapple perched on my stomach. In my
face, he's heavy and square. He's like a heavy

brown fox with a wooden shark inside.
Please don't say "like a cat." A small frenzy
of independent loamy notions. His breath
a soaking rain.

About the Author

Heather Sellers was born in Orlando, Florida, and received her PhD from Florida State University in 1992. Recipient of an NEA for fiction writing in 2001, she is also the author of *Georgia Underwater,* a collection of short stories, which won a Barnes and Noble Discover Award. Her first children's book, *Spike and Cubby: Ice Cream Island Adventure!* is forthcoming in spring 2003 from Henry Holt. *Your Whole Life,* a poetry chapbook, appeared in 1992 from Panhandler Press. Heather Sellers writes articles on running and writing, and her fiction and poetry appear in journals and anthologies. She lives in Holland, Michigan, where she raises Pembroke Welsh Corgis.

Ahsahta Press

This book is set in Apollo type with Cochin titles
by Ahsahta Press at Boise State University
and manufactured on acid-free paper
by the Boise State University Print Shop, Boise, Idaho.

AHSAHTA PRESS

2002

JANET HOLMES, DIRECTOR

SHANNON MAHONEY, EDITORIAL ASSISTANT

CAROLYN FRITSCHLE   JOSH KENNEDY

FARGO KESEY   RUSSELL KING

WILLIAM GUY MILLER   MAURA PAYNE

MATT REITER   JANELLE HIGGS, INTERN